Bell's first telephone

1866	H. G. Wells, writer, born
1867	Dominion of Canada established
1869	Suez Canal opened Sir Henry Wood, composer and conductor, born
1870	Education Act Death of Charles Dickens, writer
1871	Trade Unions legalised
1873	Sir Edwin Landseer, painter, died
1874	First practical typewriter on sale

1876	First telephone invented by Alexander Graham Bell
1878	Electric lighting introduced David Hughes invented microphone
1879	Albert Einstein, scientist, born Tay Bridge disaster
1880	Jacob Epstein, sculptor, born Elementary education becomes compulso
1881	Thomas Carlyle, historian, died Alexander Fleming, scientist, born
1887	Golden Jubilee celebration
1888	Edward Lear, artist and writer, died
1890	Opening of Forth Bridge

The Forth Bridge

Golden Jubilee decorations

1891	Free education in England
1892	Death of Alfred, Lord Tennyson (poet)
1894	Manchester Ship Canal opened
1895	Röntgen discovered X-rays
1897	Diamond Jubilee
1898	Radium discovered
1899	Boer War started Marconi sent first international wireless message
1900	Australian Commonwealth proclaimed
1901	Death of Queen Victoria

The Albert Memorial London

The Victorian age was one of great complexity and contrast, and it brought much that was new not only by way of discovery and invention but also in its great social reforms.

Queen Victoria, as both Head of State and wife and mother, had many problems to contend with.
A woman of character and determination, she dealt with them all in her own firm way. Here is the story of her life and her reign.

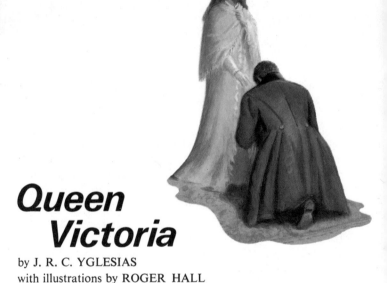

Queen Victoria

by J. R. C. YGLESIAS
with illustrations by ROGER HALL

Ladybird Books Ltd Loughborough

Kensington Palace

Princess Alexandrina Victoria was born on May 24th 1819 in Kensington Palace, London, where she spent her early life until she became Queen. At that time Kensington was a quiet district, cut off from the bustle of the main city by market gardens and country lanes. The Palace was not a very comfortable home from all accounts. In later years Victoria called it 'dreadfully dull, dark and gloomy', and referred to 'our Kensington friends, the black beetles', for it was infested with insects.

Victoria's mother was a German princess, and her father was Edward, Duke of Kent, the fourth son of King George III. The Duke of Kent's eldest brother was already reigning over the country as Regent, since George III had been blind and mentally ill for some years. The Regent was crowned George IV in 1820.

Not many months after Victoria was born, her father died heavily in debt, leaving his Duchess and her family (Princess Feodora and Prince Charles, children by her first marriage, and Victoria) penniless. She was thinking of returning to her home in Germany when her brother Prince Leopold of Saxe-Coburg came to her rescue and made her an allowance. The family lived on this until 1825 when Parliament recognised that Victoria was the probable heiress to the throne (*heiress presumptive*), and voted £6,000 yearly for her education and keep.

As a child Victoria was given to outbursts of rage and would stamp her feet and shriek to get her own way. She positively refused to learn her alphabet. Later her governess Baroness Lehzen won her over, and she grew into a well-mannered and polite little girl, who loved to ride her donkey and enjoyed Punch and Judy shows.

*Princess Victoria
with her governess, Baroness Lehzen*

During these early days Victoria's kindly uncle Leopold took a great interest in her. Until he became king of the Belgians in 1831, he lived in Surrey and it was a great treat for Victoria to visit him there.

Many of Victoria's royal relations however, both German and English, were disreputable. Her mother felt that she should have as little to do with them as possible, and kept her from seeing them. This did not please William IV, who had become king in 1830 on the death of George IV.

Victoria's mother, the Duchess of Kent 1786-1861

The Duchess was firmly supported in her view by Sir John Conroy, Comptroller of her Household, who was an ambitious man anxious for power. Victoria hated him, although she was quite friendly with his daughter to start with.

Later, when Victoria became Queen, he tried to force her to make him her Private Secretary (which was a very important position at that time) but she refused.

The Duchess brought up Victoria to rely on her for everything. Until the very moment she came to the throne, Victoria was carefully watched and supervised by her mother and governess. Everywhere she went someone accompanied her, even when walking from one room to another. She even slept in a little bed in her mother's room until she became Queen.

Yet she grew into a quiet, sensible, and affectionate young lady who showed little resentment over her treatment. She first learnt she was heiress to the throne when she was twelve, and is said to have exclaimed, 'I will be good.'

Victoria worked hard at her lessons. She had a regular timetable for each morning and afternoon learning Latin, history, geography and other school subjects. She was good at arithmetic and drawing and learnt poetry by heart. On Thursdays she had a dancing lesson, which she loved, and music on Fridays. She liked to sing, and had a good voice.

Sir John Conroy
1786-1854

In 1828 Victoria's half sister Feodora married Prince Ernest of Hohenlohe Langenburg and Victoria, then nine years old, was a bridesmaid and wore a lace dress.

After the wedding Feodora sailed for Germany. Victoria turned back to her dolls, treating them as friends. She had 132 of them, and played with them until she was nearly fourteen.

As Victoria grew into her teens, the Duchess of Kent felt that she should learn something of the country she was to rule, and become known to the people who were to be her subjects. Victoria travelled with her mother about the country in a carriage drawn by grey horses with pink silk reins, and with postboys dressed in pink silk jackets and black hats.

Princess Victoria at Cowes, with her mother

Wherever they went, they were warmly welcomed. When they visited the Isle of Wight and went sailing on the Solent (Victoria loved sailing), naval vessels were continually firing salutes to them. Victoria's uncle King William IV objected to this and ordered that in future salutes were to be fired only when the King or Queen was on board.

In spite of these holidays however Victoria led a dull life on the whole. She kept a diary which tells us a good deal about what happened in the family from day to day. Although she wrote up this journal every day throughout her long life (sometimes writing several pages even at the end of a tiring day) we only have the diaries from her early years, before she came to the throne.

William IV, 1765-1837

After her death her youngest daughter Princess Beatrice destroyed the rest, feeling they were too private for other people to read.

There were occasional very splendid parties at Windsor Castle, and sometimes her young German cousins came to stay at Kensington Palace. She first met her cousin Albert, Prince of Saxe-Coburg-Gotha, in May 1836. She liked him and wrote in her diary that he was 'extremely good looking'.

This pleased her Uncle Leopold who hoped Victoria would eventually marry Albert, who was his nephew. On the other hand the king, William IV, disliked her German relations, and wanted her to marry one of the sons of the Prince of Orange. He had tried to stop the visit of Prince Albert and his brother to Kensington.

Lord Melbourne, 1779-1848

This could have led to an awkward situation in the years ahead, but William IV died when Victoria was just eighteen years old. She was old enough to become Queen, for royal persons came of age at eighteen—three years before other people in those days.

At six o'clock in the morning on June 20th 1837 Victoria slipped on a dressing gown over her nightdress, and walked alone to her sitting room in Kensington Palace. There the Lord Chamberlain and the Archbishop of Canterbury knelt down and told her she was now Queen.

At nine o'clock that same morning Lord Melbourne the Prime Minister called. In her diary Victoria underlined the fact that she saw him *alone*—without Mama or her governess fussing her. Shortly afterwards she held her first Privy Council, which she conducted calmly and clearly. She was an instant success in court circles.

The young Queen quickly showed her will and determination. Her widowed mother, the Duchess of Kent, who had hoped to remain very much in the limelight, was put firmly in the background. Victoria immediately ordered her bed to be moved from her mother's room to a separate bedroom of her own.

Later when the household moved to Buckingham Palace her mother, the Duchess, was expected to send a note asking for permission before she visited the Queen's apartments. In contrast Victoria had great affection for Baroness Lehzen, who was asked to stay on at court to help with personal matters and with letters.

Victoria becomes Queen

Now that she no longer referred to her mother for everything, Victoria needed an adviser, and she was lucky enough to have two extremely able men at hand to help her.

One was Baron Stockmar, who was sent by her Uncle Leopold to give her advice and guidance with the many difficulties surrounding formal and social occasions of life at court. The Queen had complete confidence in him and he always placed the interest of the Queen and her country before all else.

Lord Palmerston
1784-1865

The second was Lord Melbourne the Prime Minister who with affection and skill set out to instruct her in the work of government. His tactful, worldly-wise advice gave Victoria support and courage. Lord Palmerston,

*Baron Stockmar
1781-1863*

the Foreign Secretary at this time, also played a part in her early training.

So the reign of Queen Victoria started in style. She was a great success at the formal and rather boring official dinners and receptions, although she much preferred riding and theatre-going. She loved informal parties and was always happy to stay up half the night dancing and then watch the sun rise behind St Paul's and the towers of Westminster.

All this energy and youthful enthusiasm was a wonderful change from the dull and quarrelsome court life when her uncle William IV had been king.

This happy state of affairs did not last. Her beloved Lord Melbourne had to resign because his government did not have the country's confidence, and she had a row with his successor Sir Robert Peel. Victoria did not like Peel, whose chilly smile she described as 'like the silver plate on a coffin', although later she learnt to appreciate his statesmanlike qualities and loyalty.

The row was over the Queen's ladies-in-waiting, and was really due to a misunderstanding. All the ladies were wives of men in Lord Melbourne's party (the Whigs), and Sir Robert wanted some of them replaced by ladies whose husbands were from his own party (the Tories). Victoria thought he wanted *all* her ladies replaced and she refused point-blank. Not even the Duke of Wellington (who was always sent for in moments of crisis) was able to persuade her to change her mind.

In the end Sir Robert was unable to form a government because of the difficulty. Lord Melbourne came back, and struggled on as Prime Minister until 1841.

The man who had by far the greatest influence on the Queen's life however was her husband. On 10th February 1840 Victoria married Prince Albert of Saxe-Coburg-Gotha. This handsome young man from Germany had been taken in hand and groomed for his future job by Baron Stockmar two years earlier.

Although he had been more or less chosen for her by Uncle Leopold, Victoria soon found she had fallen in love and never ceased to adore Albert. She openly doted on his 'beautiful blue eyes, his exquisite nose, the pretty mouth with delicate moustache and slight, but very slight, whiskers', as she wrote in her diary.

The Prince was gifted as well as being one of the best-looking men in Europe, and had wide interests. Even so Victoria still preferred to dance all night rather than sit and listen to his earnest discussions with authors, scientists and economists!

Prince Albert, 1819-1861

Albert refused to let her order him about. She was Queen but she was also his wife, and in those days a wife was expected to love, honour and *obey* her husband. Victoria soon realised she had married not just a handsome prince, but a man of great intelligence and virtue.

They settled down to a happy family life, and had nine children—four sons and five daughters. Princess Victoria was born at the end of 1840. Then came Edward (Bertie), Prince of Wales, who eventually succeeded Victoria as King Edward VII in 1901. As the heir to the throne, Bertie's education was very strict, but he was a disappointment to his parents since he

The Prince Consort *Princess Helena*

Princess Alice

Prince Alfred

was not clever. However he later became a popular prince both at home and overseas, and served his country well.

The royal couple's way of life set an example which had considerable influence on life and behaviour both at Court and outside it. In time the whole of the Queen's reign (1837-1901) came to be called the *Victorian* age. Yet even today *Victorian* is used to describe many different aspects of life during that period of over sixty years. It was an age of great contrasts, and more than one view is needed when surveying such a complex period.

Princess Royal

Edward
Prince of Wales

Princess
Louise

nce Arthur

The Queen
holding Princess Beatrice

Prince Leopold

For example, Victorian girls even in wealthy families had little real education. Although Florence Nightingale managed to break free and to lead her own life, few could do the same. Upper-class parents refused to let their daughters become nurses or take a job. They were taught a few social graces (*accomplishments*) in preparation for marriage, which meant a life of service to their husband's wishes. This attitude towards the education of girls and the position of women is often called *Victorian*.

Apart from this, social snobbery was everywhere to be seen. The contrast between life 'upstairs' and 'downstairs' (the servants' place) was extreme, and everyone was expected to know his or her 'place'. Thus the age of Queen Victoria has often been branded as smug and two-faced (*hypocritical*). Violent contrasts abounded between rich and poor, and between the positions of men and women in society. Despite this, the Victorian age was undoubtedly one of social progress and increasing prosperity and productivity.

Victoria herself cannot be called a hypocrite. No doubt she remained ignorant of the poverty in which most of her subjects lived, and could not always understand the reasons behind changes which her government wished to make. Nor had she the political power or the brains to match the achievements of Elizabeth I (1558-1603). However she was in a position to exercise considerably more influence on both social life and government than Elizabeth II, the present Queen.

Since Albert was keenly interested in both economic affairs and science, the monarchy during his lifetime continued to set an excellent example not so much in its family life as in its support of technical and economic progress. This progress and prosperity was there for all the world to see at the Great Exhibition in 1851.

Many of Victoria's subjects lived in great poverty

19

On May 1st 1851 Queen Victoria opened the Great Exhibition in Paxton's marvellous Crystal Palace in Hyde Park. She wrote in her diary for that day, 'This day is one of the greatest and most glorious days of our lives, with which, to my pride and joy, the name of my dearly beloved Albert is for ever associated.'

She goes on, 'The park presented a wonderful spectacle, crowds streaming through it. The day was bright and all bustle and excitement. Vicky and Bertie were in our carriage. Vicky was dressed in lace over white satin with a small wreath of pink silk roses

The Duke of Wellington 1769-1852

in her hair. Bertie was in full Highland dress. The Green Park and Hyde Park were one mass of densely crowded human beings in the highest good humour and most enthusiastic . . . The glimpse through the iron gates, the waving palms and flowers, the myriads of people filling the galleries and seats gave a sensation I shall never forget. I felt much moved.'

There are several good stories about Queen Victoria, although not all of them are true. One legend about the Great Exhibition is well known. At breakfast one day, the Queen asked Albert why he was so moody and unhappy. He explained that hundreds of sparrows had been trapped inside the Crystal Palace, which enclosed three huge elm trees. Their droppings would ruin many of the 14,000 exhibits from all over the world. No one could suggest a solution to the problem. Finally, someone thought of asking the Duke of Wellington.

In answer to a summons to Buckingham Palace, the Duke is said to have replied, 'Field Marshal the Duke of Wellington presents his humble duty to Her Majesty. The Duke of Wellington has the honour to be Commander-in-Chief to Her Majesty's Forces, but the Duke of Wellington is not a bird catcher!'

No sooner had the Duke sent the letter than he had second thoughts. He jumped on his horse, rescued the letter from the messenger, and presented himself at Buckingham Palace where he pronounced his advice: 'SPARROW-HAWKS.'

There had been other more real problems, but on the day all went perfectly. The Queen was a small figure in pink watered silk, brocaded with silver, with diamonds in her hair. Her two children Vicky and Bertie were at her side. As an eyewitness wrote: 'No one with even ordinary feeling could remain unmoved.'

A horse-bus on its way to the Great Exhibition

As the opening ceremony drew to a close, an extraordinary thing happened. A Chinese man came out of the crowd and made a deep bow to the Queen. Most people thought this mysterious figure dressed in satin must be a very important person, as he shook hands with the Duke of Wellington and others.

Since China had refused the invitation to the opening ceremony, nobody knew what to do, and the royal procession was waiting to start. So the Queen

Sir Joseph Paxton
1801-1865
designer of the Crystal Palace

24

The Crystal Palace

Sir Henry Cole, 1808-1882

ordered that he should be allowed to walk in the rear of the procession with the ambassadors from other countries.

In fact this Chinaman was called Hee Sing and was a fraud. He was a sea captain out for free publicity to draw people to visit his own show: his Chinese boat moored to the Temple pier in the Thames. When all this was discovered, everyone took it as a good joke.

One of the leaders of the procession was, of course, Sir Joseph Paxton, who had designed the gigantic greenhouse which *Punch* had christened the 'Crystal Palace'.

Although the original idea for the Great Exhibition was Sir Henry Cole's, the whole project really owed its success to Prince Albert's persistent support and encouragement. It was a resounding triumph. No less than 700,000 people cheered the Queen on her journey from Buckingham Palace to Hyde Park!

An early steam locomotive

Altogether over six million visitors flocked to it in the six months that it was open, helped by Thomas Cook's special cheap railway excursion tickets from all over England.

Many visitors saw for the first time such wonders as trains, bicycles and the electric telegraph (the telephone was not invented until the 1870s).

There were massive displays of machinery of every description, as well as silks from India, black lace from Spain, and the world-famous Koh-i-noor diamond. It was the first truly international exhibition and trade fair.

Here is an official description of the scene looking north:

'In the midst is seen the Fountain of Glass. Behind it, and also in groups near the south entrance, are beautiful tropical plants, sheltered by the elm trees which rise above them. The glitter of the falling water in the gleaming light which pours down in this part of the building, and the artistic arrangement of the objects of art and industry, make this a peculiarly attractive part of this immense structure.'

Furthermore there was a profit—of over £186,000! This was a vast fortune in 1851, and worth millions today.

Of course, the highly educated, sensible and sensitive Prince Albert saw to it that this fortune was earmarked for further education in the arts and sciences. Today you can see the result in South Kensington: the Victoria and Albert Museum, the Science Museum, the Natural History and Geological Museums, the Imperial College of Science and Technology, the Royal College of Art, the Royal College of Music and the Royal Albert Hall. And that is just the short list! Even now there is still an income of over £25,000 a year to finance educational scholarships.

The Crystal Palace itself was moved to Sydenham where it was rebuilt and opened by the Queen in 1854. For many years all sorts of festivities were held there: concerts, firework displays, Cruft's Dog Show, balloon ascents and other forms of entertainment.

Then on 30th November 1936 it was burned to the ground. There had been beacons on Sydenham Hill before—in the reign of Elizabeth I—to warn Englishmen of the approach of the Spanish Armada in 1588. But that evening in 1936, the red glow in the sky was no signal. It was a calamity.

The first rideable bicycle, made by Kirkpatrick Macmillan of Scotland in 1839

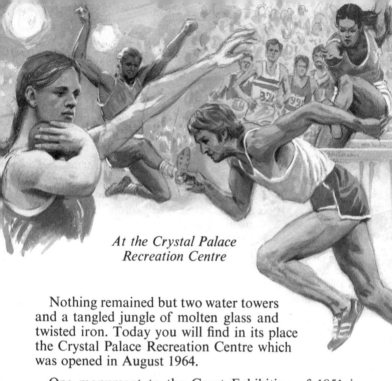

*At the Crystal Palace
Recreation Centre*

Nothing remained but two water towers
and a tangled jungle of molten glass and
twisted iron. Today you will find in its place
the Crystal Palace Recreation Centre which
was opened in August 1964.

One monument to the Great Exhibition of 1851 is
on the steps *behind* the Albert Hall. The other is the
Albert Memorial in the front—a monument which
perhaps sums up the self-satisfaction of the times.

Prince Albert himself was keenly interested in the
latest adventures and discoveries. Steamships were
beginning to cross the Atlantic faster than sailing ships;
the first bicycles were to be seen; many streets had gas
lighting. The Prince recognised the importance of
Faraday's work on electricity and by this means the
Queen later had a telegraphic link between London and
her house at Balmoral in Scotland.

The other great development was the growth of rail-
ways. By 1851 the basis of our present day railway

network was in existence. Before long the Queen's train to Scotland even had its own toilet.

So the Great Exhibition marked a high point in Victoria's long reign. Progress, wealth and luxury were there to see and the dirt, disease and poverty behind the scenes could be overlooked. Then came the shambles of the Crimean War (1854-1856), and the self-satisfaction produced by the Great Exhibition was rudely shaken.

Suddenly people were forced to face the horrors of the hospital at Scutari by vivid reports printed in *The Times* newspaper. Florence Nightingale herself sent back reports to the government on the obstruction and evil obstinacy of army officers and doctors in the Crimea.

*Fighting
in the Crimean War*

Albert's dream of peace abroad and prosperity at home was in ruins, and the Queen herself was most concerned. When Florence Nightingale returned from the Crimea, Victoria took an interest in her work.

Up to that time, nurses were described with some justification as a 'dirty, disreputable and drunken crew'. Now Florence Nightingale set about organising the training of nurses, and the administration of hospitals.

Elizabeth Blackwell was the first woman allowed to work as a doctor. Although this was in Boston, America in 1848 she was in fact an Englishwoman. Later she returned to England to continue the struggle to gain recognition for women doctors and nurses in the face of fierce and at times violent opposition.

Women were first admitted to sit the Cambridge degree examinations in 1873. They were allowed to take the degree examinations but were forbidden the award of the actual diploma. In 1890 Philippa Fawcett came top in the Cambridge mathematics examination, with

By 1880 all children between five and ten were obliged to attend school

*University education for women: the dining hall
at Girton College in the 1870s*

400 marks more than any of the men, but she was refused the usual honour award to first place (Senior
Wrangler) because she was a woman!

Not until 1948 were women allowed to receive their
degree diploma at Cambridge, although Oxford allowed
women to receive theirs in 1920.

In contrast, the education of women actually received
the approval of Queen Victoria when Bedford College
started with classes for girls in a private home, and
King's College began to train governesses.

In spite of her friendly feelings towards Florence
Nightingale and her approval of Bedford College, the
Queen did not seriously believe that women might
perhaps be allowed to vote at parliamentary elections.
Her view was 'God created men and women different,
then let them remain each in their own position.'

In another matter the Queen was a pioneer of progress and reform. She always dreaded childbirth, and when Dr Snow suggested chloroform for the birth of her eighth child (Prince Leopold) in 1853, she was glad to try it. Up to that time most doctors (all men) and many other people felt strongly that the use of gases (*anaesthetics*) in childbirth was wrong and unnatural. Now that the Queen of England had made use of chloroform all who could afford it were able to follow her example without criticism.

It was not until 1846 that gases were used during operations. Before that, a patient might get a swig of brandy while his leg was sawn off. During the 1860s Lister pioneered strict cleanliness in the operating theatre, and stressed the importance of anti-septics. Slowly others followed his lead.

These changes in attitudes were gradual.

Drawing water from the river Thames

Lord Lister, 1827-1912

It was perhaps the year of the Great Stink (1858) which stirred Edwin Chadwick and others to demand action. In that year the summer was particularly hot, and little rain fell. The stench from the river Thames was so strong that in the House of Commons they had to cover the windows with curtains soaked in chloride of lime, and anyone crossing Westminster Bridge had to hold something over his nose and mouth. Men like Charles Dickens and Charles Kingsley attacked the widespread ignorance, stupidity and stinginess in matters of public health. Kingsley wrote that in Bermondsey, people had no water to drink except from the common sewer.

It was only after the experiences of the Great Stink and numerous outbreaks of cholera that people began to recognise the connection between dirt and disease. Action followed later, when London got a proper drainage system with magnificent sewers beneath the streets.

Disraeli, the Prime Minister of the day, was aware of the great contrasts in living conditions. He thought that England was divided into two nations: the rich men about town (*Dandies*), and people living on near-starvation wages in horrible conditions (*Drudges*). In 1874 and 1875 Acts were passed to help factory workers and to improve public health. A whole range of social services which we take for granted today came into being. Horrible housing conditions and starvation were still causing some concern, but social progress was nevertheless slowly being achieved—and without the bloodshed that accompanied it in other countries in Europe during this period.

*Victoria and Albert
dance a Highland reel*

In contrast, the royal way of life was very different. Both the Queen and Albert loved Scotland, and in the 1850s Prince Albert designed a castle there. Balmoral Castle was near Braemar in the wilds of Aberdeenshire. It had granite walls, and a tower 100 foot (30.4 m) high. Inside, the walls and floors were covered with pitch pine, and Victoria's own tartan with a white stripe was in every room. There were tartan curtains, tartan chair-covers—even tartan linoleum on the floor! (Prince Albert had already designed a separate Balmoral tartan in red and grey.) Stags' antlers hung everywhere, and bronze figures of Highlanders served as lamps.

Victoria enjoyed staying at Balmoral. Some of her most vivid memories in later life centred on holidays there: Albert deer-stalking with his servant John Brown; Vicky sitting on a wasps' nest; and a torchlight dance. Victoria spent much of her time there sketching and painting and danced the Highland reels with great skill and grace.

Albert took a great interest in housing of all kinds. At the time of the Great Exhibition he had a design made for a block of model houses for working class families and this block can still be seen where it was re-erected in Kennington Park, London. Throughout Victoria's reign however the majority of people in cities lived in inescapable filth and poverty, despite the heroic efforts of a few pioneers.

Many people in cities lived in filth and poverty

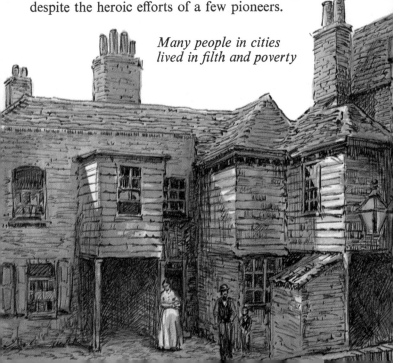

Osborne House

In those days official entertainments were usually held at Windsor Castle. There were few spectacles so imposing as the great Waterloo banqueting hall crowded with men wearing multicoloured uniforms and women dazzling in their diamonds. Stately portraits decorated the walls; the tables were loaded with gold plates.

In the midst of this official splendour, that on occasions included visits from the King of Prussia, King Louis Philippe of France and the King of Saxony, the most outstanding personality was the Queen. The little wife who had been walking with her children that morning, who had practised the piano, written up her diary, and inspected her livestock, now shone forth and impressed her distinguished guests.

On such occasions—indeed on all occasions—the Queen stuck closely to court rules and behaviour. No one was allowed to speak out of turn, and if anyone dared to take any sort of liberty in conversation at the dinner table they would receive a crushing reproof. 'We are not amused,' the Queen was heard to say when a particular remark displeased her.

At their other residence, Osborne House on the Isle of Wight, the Prince of Wales (Bertie) was once late for dinner—through no fault of his own. It is said that he stood behind a pillar wiping the sweat from his face as he plucked up enough courage to apologise to his mother. When at last he did so, she gave him a curt nod, and he then vanished behind another pillar and stayed there until dinner was over. On this occasion, he was fifty years old!

Osborne House was another home which was designed for Victoria by her beloved Albert. The royal children had a wonderful playground there, with a Swiss cottage for the boys to learn carpentry, and the girls cookery and housekeeping. The furniture was all made small enough for children, and the Queen and Prince Albert were sometimes invited to tea there.

After the end of the Crimean War in 1856, life at court was not quite so joyful or easy. Princess Vicky married the Crown Prince of Prussia and went to live abroad, and Victoria's mother, the Duchess of Kent, died in 1861. The Queen was so upset that Albert had to beg her to pull herself together and lead a normal life.

Windsor Castle

At this time Albert himself was showing signs of severe strain. He never really relaxed and daily prepared outlines of letters and government documents for the Queen to see. On top of this he took an active interest in everything that was going on, and supervised the royal households and estates—and his health suffered in consequence.

When he caught a chill in November 1861 no one was particularly alarmed. Lord Palmerston suggested a further medical opinion but was over-ruled. Two other doctors were at last called in—and found that the Prince had typhoid fever. The possibility of his death was real. In the middle of December, his children were sent for to see him for the last time before he died.

Albert died to the sound of hymns being played on a piano in the next room. It is said that Victoria uttered a shriek of such pain and anguish that it was never forgotten by those who heard it.

The Queen's grief was overwhelming, and it swamped her life for many years. According to the historian Lytton Strachey, for forty years after his death the Prince's rooms at Windsor were kept as if he were still alive. His clothing was laid out each day, and water set ready in the wash basin for him each evening.

Now she tried to cling to the past and to recapture it. Victoria in fact never threw away any of her possessions. All her dresses, muffs, parasols, bonnets and dolls were carefully put away in drawers. Each article was photographed before it was put away and the photograph put in an album with a note of where the article had been put.

So that the memory of Prince Albert would not fade, Victoria had statues put up all over the country, and his speeches published. Yet apart from Disraeli and a few others it seemed that no one really appreciated her dear Albert.

When the Queen returned to Balmoral in 1862, the summer after Albert's death, her first visit was to a widow of a cottager on the estate. Both burst into tears at the memory of their recent losses, and Victoria said she was thankful to cry with someone who knew exactly how she felt.

Victoria withdrew more and more from public life, and became so remote from the affairs of the country that for a time there was considerable resentment that she seemed to be failing the nation in her duties as Queen. 'What does she do with it?' (£385,000 a year) was the title of one pamphlet attacking her. Her private fortune was said to be five million pounds, but the monarch's wealth has always remained a close secret even today.

One consequence of her retirement from public life and affairs of state was that whereas up to the time of Albert's death the power of the crown had increased, afterwards under the Prime Ministers Gladstone, Disraeli and Lord Salisbury this power effectively declined.

The Queen however was instrumental in putting an end to one of the privileges enjoyed by the wealthy classes. When Gladstone decided to stop the purchase of military commissions, the House of Lords bitterly

W. E. Gladstone, 1809-1898
Benjamin Disraeli, 1804-1881
Lord Salisbury, 1830-1903
The Victoria Cross

40

opposed him. So he asked the Queen to make the Act law by royal warrant, and she readily agreed. She also gave her name to the highest award for bravery—the Victoria Cross. Unlike most military medals, it is awarded entirely without regard to rank: it is given simply 'for bravery'.

It was perhaps at Balmoral that Victoria could most easily remember and dwell on those happier days when Albert was around. Especially as John Brown was there. He had been Albert's personal attendant in Scotland; now he became more a constant companion than just a servant to the Queen.

Queen Victoria with John Brown

Many stories are told about John Brown's outspoken manner and his special place in the Queen's household.

One day when Victoria was sketching at Glas-allt Shiel (a small lodge not far from Balmoral), she was unable to find a table of just the right height for her drawing board. Every table in the lodge had been tried, but none would do. At last John Brown grabbed the first table he could reach among the many already rejected, and placing it before the Queen said, 'The folk canna make one for ye.' The Queen merely laughed and, accepting the position, made use of the table.

At Balmoral too she kept up the custom of listening to the bagpipes played under her window every morning from eight to nine o'clock.

Although Victoria was sharply and publicly criticised for hiding away, her critics gradually fell silent, and her popularity slowly returned. Public figures in England who attain great age tend to become popular whatever their past record may be. So it was with Victoria, and the fact that she escaped several assassination attempts helped this change of attitude towards her.

In fact there had been attempts on her life long before Albert's death. Four months after her marriage, Victoria and Albert were driving up Constitution Hill in a low carriage when a post boy named Edward Oxford fired two shots at her. He was found insane and sent to a lunatic asylum.

Two years later in May 1842, a youth named Francis fired a pistol at Victoria at exactly the same place on Constitution Hill. He was condemned to death for high treason but the Queen changed the sentence to transportation for life. The same punishment was given to Robert Pate an ex-lieutenant of the Hussars who struck the Queen in the face with a small stick in London.

There were several attempts on the Queen's life

The critical attitude towards the Queen changed most noticeably from November 1871 when the Prince of Wales became dangerously ill with typhoid fever. It was the tenth anniversary of Albert's death—and he had died of typhoid. Then Bertie made a sudden recovery, and a wave of popular sympathy swept the country.

In 1876 this little old lady with her short stout figure in folds of black velvet, muslin streamers, heavy pearls and a haughty look, became Empress of India. Her personal prestige and popularity were assured, and the monarchy took on a new look. As an institution it became more strongly established, even if it lost actual political power in the long run.

There was a further attempt on Victoria's life: in 1882 Roderick Maclean fired at her as she was entering her carriage. He was sent to a lunatic asylum.

The two main landmarks in the development of the new look of the monarchy were the Golden Jubilee of 1887, and the Diamond Jubilee of 1897. The first occasion demanded a strenuous programme of public appearances. When Victoria opened the People's Palace, she drove from Paddington to Whitechapel through streets lined with cheering crowds. On May 22nd London was illuminated when there was a special service in St Margaret's, Westminster. May 24th was the Queen's birthday. Then came the high point of the year: the Thanksgiving Service in Westminster Abbey.

The first London telephone exchange, about 1878

There was a state procession up Constitution Hill, along Piccadilly and the Embankment to the Abbey. In the procession there were kings from Denmark, Belgium and Saxony; there were crown princes and grand-dukes. There was also a special bodyguard of eighteen princes, among whom were three sons and nine grandsons and grandsons-in-law of the sovereign.

David Livingstone, explorer, 1813-1873

R. L. Stevenson, novelist, 1850-1894

Charles Dickens, novelist, 1812-1870

Isambard Kingdom Brunel, designer and engineer, 1806-1859

45

On the following day the women of England (three million subscribers) presented the Queen with £80,000 which they had collected. Part of this was spent on a statue of Prince Albert at Windsor, and the rest went to charities for women.

The years following saw a decline in her activities. She became frail, and had to walk with a stick. Later she had to be carried in a chair drawn by a pony or donkey. However, she managed to holiday abroad nearly every year, visiting Spain and France; and she went to Wales with Princess Beatrice who went down a coal mine at Llangollen. She visited Southampton and Portsmouth, and attended the Islington Horse Show as well as grand reviews at Aldershot and Spithead.

She still loved the theatre. Mr Irving's theatre company put on a show for her at Windsor—a performance of *Becket* in 1893 (Irving was knighted by her in 1895). At Balmoral the Garrick Company performed *A Scrap of Paper*. She heard the opera *Carmen* at Windsor and the Carl Rosa Opera Company's performance of *Fra Diavolo* at Balmoral.

She attended the Cowes regatta with Princess Beatrice, where they were joined by the German Emperor.

The Diamond Jubilee of 1897 was a more glorious and larger version of the 1887 celebrations. The procession and the Thanksgiving Service at St Paul's Cathedral lasted three hours, and the three cheers for the Queen which followed the playing of the National Anthem was a truly moving moment.

Alexandra, Princess of Wales, organised dinners for over three hundred thousand poor people in various parts of London, and visited them all herself. In contrast, the Duke of Devonshire gave a lavish and luxurious fancy dress ball for the exalted members of society. The Queen returned to Windsor for a family banquet, then took a much needed rest.

Diamond Jubilee celebration, 1897

The next two years were comparatively uneventful for Victoria. Her health remained good, and she went abroad for holidays as usual.

In May 1899 she laid the foundation stone of the new buildings completing the Victoria and Albert Museum—that project planned by Albert more than forty years before.

The motor car had come to stay

Bicycles now had pneumatic tyres

Then came the anxieties of the Boer War, which proved much more serious than anybody expected. The Queen showed a watchful interest in the course of the campaign; she reviewed the departing regiments and entertained the wives and children of the Windsor soldiers who had gone to the war. She sent a Christmas gift of a box of chocolates to every soldier in South Africa. She also visited Piper Findlater and Private Vickery in hospital and decorated them with the Victoria Cross for bravery in the Boer War.

In 1900 Victoria decided to visit Ireland—a land of revolution, violence and unrest that not even Mr Gladstone had been able to pacify. The Queen however admired the fighting ability of the troops she called 'my brave Irish'. In recognition of their gallantry in the Boer War she issued an order for them to wear the shamrock on St Patrick's Day, and a new regiment of Irish Guards was formed.

Apart from the public anxieties of the Boer War, the Queen had many private griefs at that time. One of her grandsons, the prince of Coburg, died in 1899, and the following year his father, the Queen's second son, also died. Then another grandson died, and Victoria's eldest daughter, the Empress Frederick, became very seriously ill. Yet another great blow fell in the death of one of the Queen's closest personal friends, the Dowager Lady Churchill.

The strain suddenly began to tell, for Victoria was now over eighty. She retired to Osborne, where her mind and body weakened slowly, and it was clear to everyone that death was approaching.

Fighting in the Boer War

When she died in January 1901, all England went into mourning. Little girls wore black; Englishmen all over the world bought handkerchiefs with black borders. On the Isle of Wight, special correspondents from every newspaper followed the procession to Trinity Pier. From there to Portsmouth warships saluted the dead sovereign as her coffin went by on the curious oldfashioned paddle-boat *Alberta*.

John Fraser of the *Yorkshire Post* described the scene at Osborne. 'The sleepy hush of the afternoon was broken by a long penetrating wail. It was the pipers playing the funeral dirge of the Black Watch. The Queen's two pipers were standing each side of the simple doorway in their Royal Scots tartan, with the dark green ribbons of their pipes streaming over their shoulders.'

The last scene of all was at St George's Chapel, Windsor. It was a solemn and gorgeous scene with statesmen, warriors, ambassadors and envoys extraordinary and goldbreasted Privy Councillors in their colourful costumes. One man only wore a simple evening dress with no ornament and no decoration – Mr Choate, Ambassador from the United States.

After the Order of the Burial of the Dead, the choirboys sang, 'I know that my Redeemer liveth.' Bertie, King Edward VII, stood at the head of the coffin, and on his right was his Imperial nephew, William, King of Prussia, German Emperor.

Throughout the next day—Sunday—the body of the Queen remained in the Albert Memorial Chapel, and on Monday was interred beside Prince Albert.

So ended the reign of Queen Victoria. With it, the already creaking period of prosperity and peace also ended. The contrasts were still there; and no real balance sheet can be drawn up. So we must continue to use the word *Victorian* to describe the many different aspects of that long reign from 1837 to 1901.

Queen Victoria in old age,
the future king Edward VII behind her

INDEX